The Teachings of Inner Ramana

Other works by Regina Dawn Akers

The Holy Spirit's Interpretation of the New Testament (NTI), published by O Books of London, available from www.amazon.com

The Holy Spirit's Interpretation of the New Testament (NTI) - AUDIO, available from www.audiblespirit.com

The Teachings of Inner Ramana

Received by

Regina Dawn Akers

Diamond Clear Vision

Quincy, MA

Library of Congress Control Number: 2010936490

ISBN: 978-0-9829225-3-8

Published and distributed by *Diamond Clear Vision*

140 Adams St.

Quincy, MA 02169

www.diamondclearvision.com

Email - info@diamondclearvision.com

- - - - -

If you are unable to order this book from your local bookseller, you may order directly from the publisher. Special quantity discounts for organizations are available.

- - - - -

Audio by Audible Spirit

5114 Balcones Woods Dr., Suite 307-418

Austin, TX. 78759

Phone – (707) 901-7734

Email – orders@audiblespirit.com

Graphic design by Philip Frisk

Product layout design by Larry Seyer

Printed by Shanghai KS Printing Co., China

The Teachings of Inner Ramana

Contents

Introduction

By Regina Dawn Akers

I began listening to Ramana Maharshi as an inner teacher on February 12, 2009. Here is how Ramana came to be my teacher:

First of all, I had never been a student of his and I never imagined that I would be. I knew next to nothing about Ramana Maharshi. But around January 25th, I was feeling that I had hit some kind of plateau and I was not progressing on the spiritual path like I had in the past. In fact, I felt I was losing the connection with Holy Spirit and ego was growing stronger in my mind. So I said a prayer and asked Holy Spirit to send me something that would take me to the next step.

On January 30th I felt spontaneously guided to buy a book by Ramana Maharshi. The book came within a few days but I did not feel guided to read it. I glanced at it, but found it very difficult to understand. I had no real attraction to his teaching.

Ramana's book sat on the coffee table near where I meditate for a week or so, then on February 12th the picture of Ramana that is on the cover of the book seemed to come alive. It seemed to breathe. I ignored this for a bit, but the feeling of aliveness kept growing. So finally I asked, "What do you want to tell me?" And the "Commentary on Mind," the first message given on February 12th, 2009 came. He seems to have come in answer to my prayer that I be taken to the next step.

All of the messages given by the Inner Ramana are archived and taught at www.reginadawnakers.com.

Throughout this book, Inner Ramana is the teacher. Regina Dawn Akers is the student or questioner.

Commentary on Mind
February 12, 2009

The mind is not constant. The concerns of the mind for one day may be completely different than the concerns for another. If all of the concerns for one day are written down, it may be seen that concerns and imagined solutions conflict with one another, so that no true peace can be found with the mind. The solution of concerns creates new concerns. And so again, there is no peace with the mind.

This is why one must step away from the mind to find peace. Peace cannot be found with the mind.

Stepping away from the mind is as simple as losing interest in it. When the mind chatters, it chatters because you are listening. As you lose interest in what it has to say, because you know its answers are not your answers, the chattering of mind shall fade away.

Mind cannot be ignored entirely. Mind is like a tool that must be used if one is to experience this world in any way. Mind is the tool of perception. Perception can only be experienced through mind. But this is not the same as saying that mind controls perception or that one must listen to the chattering or problems and solutions of mind.

Think of mind as a filter. This filter enables one to see objects where there is light. This filter enables one to distinguish differences where there are none. It enables one to communicate using symbols that represent something else. Without the mind, one would be unable to experience the world. But this does not mean that one must be subject to the mind.

The mind, when believed and taken seriously, seems to define reality. But as I have just shown, the mind does not define reality. It places a veil of perception over reality so reality can be experienced in a new way. This means that the mind is a trickster or illusionist, and that which it creates is purely illusion. To believe the mind is to believe illusion. To think illusion is reality is to be completely deluded.

Again I emphasize that belief in illusion, or the process of being deluded, comes from believing the mind.

This must mean then, that the process of awakening is also the process of learning not to believe the stories of the mind.

As a filter, the mind can be used to see and experience illusion without believing it. This experience comes from maintaining knowledge that is beyond the mind. It can also be said that this knowledge is before the mind. This knowledge exists now, within the Self, at a depth that is below and at a height that is above the mind. In other words, the knowledge is always accessible and it takes only desire to remember and realize this knowledge.

I ask you to practice.

I have given you a mantra, "I am that I am." I ask you to practice this mantra to the utmost of your ability. This means practice it as much as you remember. This mantra shall access knowledge and bring it back to you (similar to the way a computer command can access a saved file and open it into memory.)

And at the same time, I ask you to practice surrender. Surrender does not see the mind's problems and solutions as important. It puts aside the mind's stories and listens in the moment for direct communication from me.

Through the use of mantra and surrender, the mind becomes a tool that is used. It is no longer a tool that acts as user. Perception is still experienced, but the filter is cleansed of false ideas so that perception is experienced with clarity. This is also called true perception, because it is not cluttered with ideas of illusion. Perception is seen and experienced, but truth is realized and remembered, so that the one experiencing and communicating through the filter cannot be referred to as deluded.

The Purpose of Surrender

February 13, 2009

We are going to learn *not* to listen to the mind. We are going to learn not to listen to the mind, first, by listening to another Voice, which speaks through the mind, but does not speak from mind, for mind or with mind. This Voice can see mind and it sees all that mind sees when it looks through mind, but it is outside of mind, so it is not confused about reality. This Voice speaks through the filter, so its knowledge can be interpreted for those who still listen to and believe the filter, but this Voice is not confused by the filter that it uses.

This is the purpose of surrender: To be guided by a Voice that is not confused when you are still at a place in mind . . . a level of vibration . . . where you can be confused or not confused. In this state, the only way to ensure you have not stepped into confusion is to consistently check with the Voice that isn't confused, and ask it what you are to do now.

The question, "What am I to do now?" is not just a question about activity, although physical guidance is within the realm of guidance given by this Voice.

The question, "What am I to do now?" also includes:

- How am I to see this?
- How shall I listen?
- How shall I be now?
- What am I to hear?
- What would you have me know?
- What is my perspective as given by you?
- How shall I respond?
- What shall I think?
- What would you have me see in me that I am not seeing?

The question, "What am I to do now?" is a fully inclusive question in which the one who perceives himself as having a separate body and separate mind turns that seemingly separate entity over fully and entirely so that no seeming independence can be said to remain as separate and on its own existence. This is the idea of being fully plugged in and running on the power of another or one that is greater, but this perception of running on another is only held to as long as the perception of possible independence persists. Once that perception has died, the possibility of perceiving another to surrender to has died also.

The Purpose of Surrender, Part Two

February 16, 2009

The mind creates experience that is not real. It is illusion or fantasy, and it is created for the purpose of enjoyment or pleasure. But when the mind forgets reality and sees the unreal as real, fear is a necessary component.

The mind is afraid because the unnatural is not natural. The mind that has forgotten reality knows that something is wrong, but it does not know what that is. It projects stories in an effort to give itself a reason for its fear, but it cannot find the answer it seeks because it is looking in the wrong direction. Its fear does not come from its own projections, and so solutions to those projections cannot end the fear.

Fear comes simply from not knowing reality. Therefore, the only answer to fear is to let go of what is false and to remember reality as true.

Discarding the world is as simple as remembering that it isn't true. This is as simple as living from within instead of from without.

One who is forgetting the world takes his cues from within. When observed, he may seem to respond to without. He may even seem to respond to his thoughts, which are still without, but this is only if you observe him from without. Without will see without. Within will see within.

One who is awakening to truth is also discarding the world, which includes discarding his thoughts about the world, so this one is learning to take all of his cues from within . . . from beyond the clouds of his thoughts.

True perception is a bridge. Guidance is a bridge. To feel that one is awakened or living outside of mind when one is experiencing perception or guidance is an error. To say that one lives outside of mind when one experiences perception is to remain deluded.

But to listen to guidance and to say that one is guided by mind outside of mind is not to be deluded. It is merely to describe the experience in words. It is merely to recognize that mind is needed to experience perception, but guidance is the echo of knowledge filtered through mind.

One who listens to guidance may be said by others to be awakened, but this one will only say he is realized, because he realizes truth even as he experiences perception. He listens to knowledge because he knows that one who sees perception cannot truly see, but one who is not attached can be guided. Non-attachment and realization are one. Seeing truth is to be awakened.

World-focused thought is always an error. It is attachment. Therefore, it is dreaming or remaining deluded.

To help people with world-focused thoughts by providing world-focused solutions is assisting one to dream. Therefore, the Awakened One, who has accepted the role of continuing the awakening, will not assist in world-focused concerns by providing world-focused answers. The Awakened One will assist world-focus by observing the filter with the one who has a desire to awaken.

When one is not world-focused, guidance within the world occurs naturally. Non-attached activity within perception is not a hindrance to awakening. Attached activity is a means of clinging to the dream.

Instructions for Using the Mantra

February 17, 2009

Today let's talk about the practice of the mantra and how this practice is best used to quiet the mind.

The quieting of mind is essential to awakening (or to realization of Self). This is because thinking acts as a blanket that covers Self and hides it completely from view. Therefore it makes sense that if one is to realize Self, he must remove the blanket.

This is the purpose of the mantra. When it is not used fully to remove the blanket completely, it can still be used partially to enable one to have peeks beneath the blanket. These peeks are helpful . . . valuable, in fact . . . to the realization of Self, because they help one to realize the goal in a very real way. This increases the desire to strive for the goal through devotion and practice.

So our purpose is to quiet the mind as much as possible. And it is also our purpose to quiet the mind in a sincere way, which is different than quieting the mind through denial or fear.

Let me now teach you how to use the mantra.

The first rule of following the practice of mantra is: ***You will use the mantra as often as you remember.*** Try to avoid remembering the use of mantra and still choosing not to use it. Resistance may come into the mind in this way. The reminder of mantra may appear and then a thought that you are "too busy in the moment to do it properly and so it is better to do it later." That is nonsense. If the reminder of the mantra has come into the mind now, then now is the perfect time to do it.

The second rule of practicing the mantra is: ***It can be done with eyes open or eyes closed.*** Eyes closed can help to bring full focus to the mantra, but if one is involved in an activity such as driving when the reminder comes to do the mantra, the restrictions brought about by the activity are not limiting to the usefulness of the mantra.

Rule three is to ***practice the mantra with love and devotion.*** Say the mantra from the Heart. I have told you that the mantra is a gift of awakening. Cherish it as a very precious gift. In the moments that you give to the mantra, give with the love that you would give to the most precious of all gifts.

The mantra is a practice of devotion (love) and discipline (consistency), but let the Heart focus on love. Discipline is the decision to practice the mantra every time you remember, but love is the way to practice.

Rule four is that you ***be willing to stay in the stillness of the mantra.*** Before the reminder of the mantra appeared, the mind may have been busy with world-based thoughts. You are not taking a break from thoughts when you say the mantra, and then quickly returning to the world. You are using the mantra to let go of thoughts because they have no real importance. You are releasing your attachment to illusion and returning the mind to the Heart, which is peace and stillness and willingness to listen only to me.

This is the practice of the mantra. Done in love and with great and joyous willingness, the benefit to realization is also great.

The mantra is "I am that I am."

The Circus and the Meadow
February 18, 2009

The mind is very active. If you watch it you will see it is much like acrobats in a circus. It is always jumping this way and that, bending and turning, and it has some very amazing moves. But it is a circus. It is not at all representative of reality. In fact, it is a complete distraction from reality. You will never notice reality if you remain focused on the circus act of the mind.

So now our primary interest is to lose interest in the mind. It is very tempting to pay attention to it, just as a great circus act catches the desire of your attention. But deep within you there is a desire that wants to settle within the meadows that surround the circus tent more than you want to be caught up in the circus.

So we are turning our attention from the ups and downs and spins and tumbles of the mind to the everlasting tranquility of the meadows. (And there is much happening in the meadows too! But it is real, which is much different than the circus.)

True stillness cannot be achieved by quieting the mind through meditative practices for part of the day and then being wrapped up in the stories of the mind the rest of the day. This is like running in and out of the circus. Sure, you may experience and know the tranquility of the meadow, but you are still addicted to the hype of the circus. The circus remains real for you. You will never be free through partial abidance. Only total abidance can be totally freeing.

The mind is going to want to think. You are going to be drawn back into the circus. But an inner response to this desire as soon as you notice it is most helpful to awakening. The inner response is one that turns your attention from the noise of the circus to the quiet love for the meadow.

This is the purpose of the mantra I have given you. It consistently and repeatedly throughout the day turns your attention from the circus and back toward the meadow, which is your truest of desires.

Wear the mantra like a layer of clothing. Practice it throughout the day, whatever you are doing. The mantra cannot be practiced too much as we are teaching the mind through desire to remain still.

Surrender is a means of living within the world while releasing your attachment to the circus.

The body remains, as do the senses of sight, smell, hearing, taste and touch. In this way, interaction with the world is non-avoidable as long as the image of the world remains in the mind. Attachment to the world continues to build the image of the world and all of the false concepts it represents. Non-attachment through surrender releases the world within the mind, which allows a slowing of its images and a fading of illusion from sight.

Attachment keeps the world going. The circus is in full swing. Non-attachment lets it fade until only the meadows remain.

Sitting with me for hours each day is also helpful, because my presence and my certainty strengthen your resolve. In this way, I ask you to be my student.

When the mind is not occupied in the silence of the mantra, let it be used for the purpose of surrender. This way the mind is always used purposefully, and one's toes will wiggle and curl delightfully as they feel the coolness of the meadow's ground beneath them.

Surrender of the common practices of the day, such as what to eat and what to wear, when to sleep, what to say and when to speak; surrender of such practices is letting go of ego, because ego indulges its self, its sense of self, through ordinary practices such as these.

Even after following a practice of surrender, mind will want to think about that practice. It will want to be proud for listening and following, or it will want to analyze the meaning of the act you were guided to follow, or it will want to imagine the results, the impact or the next step. All of this is returning to the circus, so when you see the mind acting in this way, practice the mantra to return the mind to the meadow.

Question for the Inner Teacher*: What do I do with this strong resistance to the practices you are asking me to keep?*

Answer: Understand that all resistance comes from your willingness to listen to resistance before. It is an echo from the past that is being picked up and heard now. To listen to it again is like shouting into a cave again. The echo will only return.

One may stand at the mouth of the cave and shout at his own echo forever and the echo will not die. It will only return more frequently, and if his shouts get louder, the echo will grow louder too.

The way to end the feeling of resistance is to stop shouting into the cave.

Be gentle with yourself. When you are feeling resistance, quietly and gently practice the mantra anyway. This practice will not hurt you. And because you are passing on the temptation to shout into the cave, the echoes are beginning to die, and practice will come more easily in the future.

Looking at the False "I" Thought
February 19, 2009

It's time to go beyond everything you've learned.

Everything you've learned has been helpful. It's been helpful toward willingness to take this next step. But without the step that we are taking together now, all that you've learned serves no real purpose toward awakening.

First we have to notice the false "I" and then we must relinquish it by not listening to its chatter anymore.

It is one thing to tell you that a separate individual "I" exists in your thinking and this "I" is an obstacle to realizing the truth about yourself. It is another thing for you to see and notice this "I" for yourself. As you look, you will notice that "I" exists as thought. You will notice that it reinforces itself through the constant chatter of the mind. Every story the mind tells reinforces the concept of "me." Every little thought, no matter how subtle, reinforces the individual concept it has of itself.

Today we will continue to practice the mantra and surrender as a means of quieting the mind and detaching from thought. These two practices are key to your awakening, and we will not abandon them as "just a step."

But to reinforce your willingness and desire to practice the mantra and surrender with the full devotion of your Heart, we are going to embark on another step of learning. We are going to look exactingly on the core message of the mind.

Today when you notice the chatter in the mind, quiet the mind with the mantra. And then with the coolness (maturity) of the quieted mind, look back at what the mind was telling you while you were listening to its chatter. Look for the "I" or "me" in the story or thought. Discover how the tricks and tumbles of the mind . . . in whatever direction it was turning in the moment . . . ; notice how it was telling you about "I" or "me" separate from everything else.

This is the key attachment in the mind. All other attachments are brought about to support and reinforce this one. So as we let go of seeming specific attachments through surrender and through quieting the mind, we are really letting go of one key attachment. I will call that the false identity "I" or "me."

Surrender is a means of detaching from the false "I" because surrender acts in the world without belief or interest in the mind's stories and ideas, which are the stories and ideas that uphold the idea of "I."

It is important to notice that this "I" is fully supported by thought.

"I am not that," can be a helpful inner response when the mind is insisting through its stories and ideas that you are what you are not. After refusing to accept the mind's thoughts as your truth, you can humbly and with desire return the mind to the mantra and surrender, which are the path . . . the moving walkway . . . back into the remembrance of your truth.

It is important to realize that belief in the mind writes the script of the world. Therefore, surrendered-action without belief does not write a script. In this way, it ultimately frees one from the illusion of the world.

The Importance of Practice
February 20, 2009

Much of what you do comes from the ego. Let me define "ego" for you since all words can have varying meanings.

"Ego" is the belief in the false identity "I."

So when I say that much of what you do comes from the ego, I mean that you are being driven or moved by that belief in the mind. That is the same as saying you are listening to and believing thoughts or stories in the mind. And this is belief in illusion.

We've already agreed that our purpose now is not to believe the mind. This is what I call non-attachment. Non-attachment is not believing the mind. Complete non-attachment is realization.

So if much of what you do comes from attachment or believing the mind, achieving non-attachment must come from *doing differently*, and this is the purpose of surrender.

When you ask me for guidance in the moment, you are giving willingness to detach from ego . . . or belief in false "I" . . . and realize true Self through non-attachment.

To try to understand awakening while the false concept "I" is in place can be very frightening, because as false "I" stretches beyond itself to understand what is being taught, it finds it is not there. To the one who defines himself by this false thought, absence of "I" appears as death.

Living without "I" is the answer to this fear. This is how true perception or guidance becomes a bridge.

Some people want to understand awakening before committing themselves fully to it. They want to ensure they can understand that awakening is safe and is not death. But I would ask these ones to ask themselves, "Who wants to understand awakening?" If they make this inquiry they may discover it is attachment to the false "I" that wants to feel safe. In this way, to continue to seek spiritual knowledge or understanding is to remain attached to the false concept "I."

It is much better to use your time in the practice of the mantra and surrender. You will awaken faster through these practices than through asking questions about awakening.

The power that makes the universe turn is you. This is not a vain statement. This is merely absolute truth. The world and all that you experience . . . your universe of objects and relationships and reactions . . . comes from you. It comes from your belief in these experiences and your thoughts about them.

This is why . . . in brief . . . .why the world fades from sight as you practice the mantra and surrender. The world comes from your attachment to your thoughts. As you detach from these thoughts, there is no more power to make a world.

Jesus told you that you would begin to see light around objects, and this is the beginning of true vision.[1] I tell you that the truth is one, and the appearance of objects occurs only because you believe the mind.

By listening to me through surrender you detach from your belief in objects and a world, and you allow them to fade.

By practicing the mantra you still the mind, and you are no longer adding to the power that creates the world of objects seen and experienced.

1 – A Course in Miracles Workbook for Students, Lesson 15

The Importance of Practice, Part Two

February 21, 2009

Surrender is a practice I will continue to emphasize, because it is one of the most helpful of all spiritual practices. One may argue that surrender is not the only path of awakening, but this is more of an emphasis than a truth.

The only path of awakening is to deny the false. And the false must be denied completely.

Surrender is a means of doing this while still moving about in the world. Without surrender, one may deny the world by withdrawing from it. This is also a path that has worked.

The enlightened person who realizes Self while still experiencing a body does not experience independence. The belief in independence, or the idea of ego, has died for this one or he would not be realized.

As there is no idea of independence, there is also no idea of deciding for himself. The enlightened one who lives in a fully realized state lives and acts, moves and speaks, according to a script that is fed to him in the moment. This script comes from the One for the highest purposes of the One, so the enlightened person does not feel separate from the script-maker, nor does he feel he is making decisions for himself. He follows in joy and realization.

Is it surrender when the enlightened one follows this script? Since there is no other, who would he surrender to? And yet it is following, just as surrender contains the idea "to follow."

Some would call this script karma. And others use the term "script," but whenever there is a feeling of victim associated with the idea "karma is established" or "the script is written," one has not yet realized the maker of the script.

This is also why the questions of free will and destiny seem to conflict when looked at through the human psyche. The human psyche cannot understand the compatibility of destiny and free will, because the human psyche sees itself as independent and has not realized the greater truth of Self.

You are not separate from the script-maker. This is the absolute truth I shared with you yesterday. But as long as your mind believes the thought of independence . . . the false concept "I" . . . this is a point you will easily become confused on. Therefore it is a point I ask you not to think about, but merely to trust.

And I ask also, since you cannot understand how you make a script, that you refrain from script-making by quieting the mind and by living or acting based upon surrender.

If you follow the practice of mantra and surrender, and refrain from "thinking for yourself," you also refrain from making a script that includes a false-concept self. Since this self is only part of a script and not part of reality, ceasing to make it also allows it, as an idea, to fade. This is part of awakening, because this is non-attachment to a false "I." Non-attachment to the false lays the way . . . opens the skies . . . to allow realization of the truth.

True Understanding Comes from Seeing
February 22, 2009

Intellectual questioning and intellectual answers cannot give sight to the blind. You cannot tell a blind man what blue is when the blind man does not know of color. You may tell him of the coolness of blue and compare it to the fiery hotness of red, and although this may give him some idea of the difference of color, it will not answer his question, "What is blue?"

Likewise, I cannot answer your questions regarding the nature of reality. You must choose to see these answers for yourself. But I can tell you about the nature of your blindness, and therefore how to find a cure. When your blindness is healed, you will see, for sight is only natural to an un-blinded man.

Exposing the "I" Thought

February 23, 2009

Let's talk for a moment of the power of the "I" thought. This power that I speak of is merely the power of distraction or deception, and it has no true power or effect over the Heart. For the true Heart knows itself and cannot be affected by distraction or deception. But the "I" thought has the power to keep you distracted from your Heart, so that you forget for a time . . . possibly for a long, long time . . . what it is that you want and what it is that you are not.

What you want is to know Self.
What you are not is the "I" thought.

I feel I must say this again and bring your attention to what I have said, because as long as you are deceived by this one deception, you cannot know the truth of Self. This deception blinds you to your true nature. I say again, this deception blinds you to your true nature. And this deception is the false identity "I."

"What am I?" is a good question to ask. The mind can come up with a myriad of answers to satisfy itself with an identity . . . an image . . . that says, "This is what (or who) I am." But each of the mind's answers fall short of truth, because each of the mind's answers provide an identity-thought that sets you apart from others. Here are some examples:

- I am man/woman.
- I am worker/not a worker.
- I am a minister.
- I am one who sits in stillness.
- I am a family man/mother.
- I am one who has renounced family and possessions.
- I am a child/adult.
- I am a person/dog/tree.
- I am an object or preferred idea.
- In short, I am separate from other objects or less preferred ideas.
- I can identify myself separate from other selves.

This is the "I" thought.

Relinquishment of the "I" thought also means relinquishment of all ideas of identity. This includes relinquishment of "I am one who does not think of 'I.'"

One delay thought that the "I" thought provides as a means of survival is, "I must change my circumstances in order to do the work necessary to relinquish thoughts of 'I.'" But I would encourage one to ask, "Who must change circumstances?" Certainly if one asks this question, he will find that "I" who feels individual and separate from this circumstance feels the circumstance must change. Upon discovering this, one can see he is being tempted by the distraction of the "I" thought, and he can choose to return to his mantra instead.

Every circumstance is appropriate for letting go of the false "I" thought, because every circumstance is being experienced now, and now is always the time to turn the attention from "I"-thinking back to concentrated stillness in the mind.

Concentrated stillness is not "I"-thinking. It is not even "I am still."

You do not know the nature of the Self, because you believe fully that you are the "I" in thought. But what you are is beyond thought. Knowing this Self is the goal we seek.

Question for the Inner Teacher*: I have one question that I do not feel clear on. What of those who have been given the mantra "I am that I am?" Is that not the "I" thought?*

Answer: "I am that I am," although it contains the word "I," is not the "I" thought. "I" is a symbol, but it is not an identity thought. When the symbol is attached to the false identity, it has the power of separating within the mind . . . within perception. When false identity is not attached to the "I" symbol, the symbol does not separate.

It is the "I" thought that wants to judge and separate the symbol "I" from all other symbols. Then "I" can be one who does not use "I," for example. But this is not the same as relinquishment of the "I" thought.

One who uses the mantra "I am that I am" can feel the mind is being moved away from the "I" thought (which is identity with a limited concept of "I"). Therefore, the mantra is helpful and is not a detriment simply because of the use of the symbol "I."

Exposing the Attachment to Mind

February 24, 2009

It is not my function to explain the Self to you. The Self is not to be understood. Rather, it is my function to help you see how you hide the Self from yourself, so you can choose to let go of the action of hiding it.

You have identified with the mind, which is an error, because you are before the mind. I want you to see, first, that you have identified with the mind. For you cannot question and go beyond something you do not see. First you must see it. Then you can choose to question, "Is this true?"

We have spoken of your resistance to surrender, and certainly this is something you have noticed by now. May I ask . . . When you do not want to surrender, what does not want to surrender? Isn't it the mind? Aren't there thoughts in the mind about what you want to do? And don't you want to listen to these thoughts?

Why do you want to listen to the thoughts in the mind? Isn't it because you are identified with the mind as if it is you? Don't you believe that the mind's thoughts are like the skin of you and to be separated from what you think you want is as terrible as separating the body from its skin?

Look at this for a moment and question, "Do I think I am my mind?"

Don't you see that this is true?

Clarity on Purpose
February 25, 2009

Now that the attachment to mind has been exposed, you see the obstacle to know Self. The obstacle is no longer hidden.

You also see the value of the mantra and the practice of surrender. Neither of the practices are about the practices in themselves. In both cases, the practices are used as tools or means to gently break the attachment to mind.

The mantra and surrender are gentle means that allow you to break the attachment to mind while living the life that mind has given you to live. This is like being set free from bondage, and yet no outer changes were required for freedom to be realized. (This does not mean there will not be outer changes. It simply means it is realized that the outer changes did not result in freedom.)

We've spoken before that mind cannot be ignored entirely. Mind is a filter that allows one to experience the world. But there is a difference between listening for cues or communication through mind and being identified with it, just as there is a difference between using a hammer and being identified with one. You would not identify yourself with a hammer even if you use it all day every day as your primary means of livelihood. Likewise, it is an error to be identified with mind.

The best way to break identification with the mind is to cease the activity of listening to it as if it is you. As we have said before, you must lose interest in it. And yet remember that it is a tool that will occasionally be used to contact you and move you, so do not be afraid of it. Be willing to keep mind open, always ready to receive communication and guidance from me.

("Me" is a symbol that is helpful for communication, but there is no true guide waiting to give commands or guidance to a surrendered servant. There is no "other." All guidance comes from the unified field of mind. All guidance is guidance from One.)

When you are not identified with mind and you are not attached to specific activities or ideas in the world, you are free to listen through mind like one who receives knowledge from the movements of the wind. You can trust that where you are placed and what you are asked to do is always in the best service . . . in perfect harmony . . . with the whole. You are never disconnected, and you are always at peace with it.

Cues can come before mind. What I mean to say is, an idea of movement or action may come through mind followed immediately with identification to mind and more thinking about the cue. When one comes to notice the difference between the unattached, impersonal cue and the attached identification and thinking that follows, one will also see immediately when to return the mind to silence while still following the impersonal prompt or cue.

The mantra is helpful because it silences the mind while leaving it open for cues.

Resistance to the easy life of following comes from fear that identity with the mind is you. And yet, identity is just an idea, and so it cannot be you.

One must realize that as long as you have concern for doing or the outer ideas of the world, one is not focused on Self. One cannot know Self if one will not immerse himself in Self. And one cannot be immersed in mind and the concerns of the world and know Self too.

But if one will take the time to be immersed in Self, one will know Self, and one will be guided in the world. There is no loss when one chooses to abide in Self.

Your focus now is to lose interest in the mind. Do not worry that you will miss a cue as it travels to you on the wings of the wind. Always there will come another breeze to guide you. Your function is to abide in Self by breaking attachment to the mind.

Clarity on Practice

February 26, 2009

Question for the Inner Teacher: *Teacher, I would like it if you would speak to me more about resistance to the practice of mantra and surrender.*

Answer: Resistance is not your true nature. When you think you are experiencing resistance you are forgetting your Self and identifying with the mind. Ask, "Who resists this practice?" Notice the mind resists, and if you believe you resist, then you believe you are the mind.

The stillness and peace within do not resist. Ask the question then, "What am I?" and await the true answer of the Heart.

Question for the Inner Teacher: *For the last 24 hours, since listening to you last, my mind has been a mad house. But the second I sat to listen to you this morning, the madness melted. It literally dissolved in your presence. Would you please speak on this with a purpose of teaching me to surrender?*

Answer: You recognize that the ego dissolved in my presence. This is always the case. Darkness disappears . . . literally disappears . . . when the light shines on it.

The question is not "Does surrender work," for obviously it does. The question is, "What is surrender?"

The mind thinks it's you, and you think you are the mind. When the mind learns what I teach and tries to practice it, that is not surrender, because that is holding onto the idea that you are the mind and the mind is you, and through the efforts of the mind you can do this. The mind can never do this. It cannot take you to realization of Self because false identity with mind is the obstacle to realizing Self.

If the efforts of surrender are not in the moment, quieting the mind and warming the Heart, it is because you are not in that moment surrendered. You are listening to mind.

Surrender is a decision to put aside mind completely. It is recognition that the answer cannot come from the mind. It is quitting the mind and turning to higher knowledge for guidance without any lingering thoughts that through the ideas and education of mind, you know what to do.

Watch for the thought that through the ideas and education of mind . . . including prior education that has come from me . . . you know what to do. Whenever you listen to the thought that you know what to do because of prior learning stored in the mind, you are not surrendered to me. Surrender has no prior knowledge it can depend on. Surrender must always turn to me.

In this, you will feel the Heart open and the ego dissolve.

"What am I to do now?" Ask this question 1000 times per day, and you are beginning to learn the true practice of surrender.

Because the thinking mind is attached to you like skin, you must allow me to become your second skin. See me as your newer, stronger and more vital skin. See the ego's skin as becoming old, worn and useless. Let me be your second skin by asking me what you are to think, how you are to see, and what you are to do. Do not depend on prior learning or knowledge. Do not judge me by the mind's standards. To do this is still to rely on the old skin. Stick to the new skin, and let it guide you freshly . . . surprisingly . . . in each new and untarnished moment.

The purpose of the mantra is to still the mind. It is like turning a radio dial from the egoic radio station to the station that I am. Both stations use the mind to communicate, just as two radio stations use one receiver. But the egoic station believes you are the radio receiver. My station realizes the radio is only a means of communication.

The purpose of the mantra is to change stations . . . to tune in to me. And repeated use of the mantra will help you to stay tuned in to me. But once our frequency of communication has been established, you link to me . . . become one with me . . . by asking me to guide your every thought and action.

Question for the Inner Teacher: *Teacher, may I summarize how I am to use the tools you have given me, and will you correct any misunderstandings that I have?*

Answer: Yes.

Question: *When the mind is active as me . . . or when I think I am the mind . . . I use the mantra to return to the Heart and my remembrance of you. And then I ask what I am to do, and I remain surrendered by asking this question 1000 times per day.*

If I find resistance and I believe that I am resistant, I question the source of the resistance. Then I remind myself that I am not the mind through asking, "What am I?" When I am free of identification with the mind, I say the mantra to reconnect with you, and then I surrender fully by asking, "What am I to do?"

Inner Teacher: Yes.

Questioner: *I see I have not been doing that. Thank you.*

Inner Teacher: Your lesson for today is one of continued looking at who you think you are. This is the false identification "I" thought or false identification with the mind. Both ideas are the same and both ideas are false. This idea is the root of all illusion, and so this one thought must be relinquished if one is to be free of delusion.

An idea is relinquished by looking at it, by challenging it, and by seeing it is false. Since the idea of ego has been deeply learned through repetition, deep and consistent unlearning must result.

So now we will add the practice of questioning to practices I have already taught you.

Question for the Inner Teacher*: How shall we add the practice? I am afraid it is too many practices and I will forget.*

Answer: That is how we shall add the practice. When you notice yourself having an "I" thought, question who "I" is. This is so you will notice the identity attachment. You cannot relinquish what you fail to notice. But when you notice it, you will relinquish it, because this desire (false identity) is not your true Heart, and you are listening to your true Heart now.

How to Awaken from the Dream
March 3, 2009

Today I would like to talk to you about expectations and imagination, and help you to see that expectations are imagination so you may choose to relinquish all expectations as mere foolishness.

I have already told you that I cannot tell you of your Self. I cannot, and yet you want to continue to speak of the Self and talk about what the Self is. You want to say that you know when someone is truly abiding in Self and when he is not. You want to speak of your experiences with Self and say, "I have some taste of the experience of Self." But I would ask you to stop and look at this discussion of Self and this asking about Self and this sharing of what "I" know about Self and ask, "Who is the 'I' that is thinking about Self, making decisions about Self and agreeing or disagreeing on what Self is?"

We have already seen that attachment to mind is the obstacle that blocks the realization of Self. Now we must continue to look at how you are attached to mind. Questioning about Self, discussion about Self and "I" experiences with Self all continue the attachment to mind, which means that although they seem to be sincere seeking of Self, they are holding onto the identity that blocks your knowledge of Self.

***Question for the Inner Teacher**: I am watching my mind now. I do not remember ever feeling such a strong desire to think while writing with the inner teacher. My mind wants to think about when I talk about Self as the attachment to mind and when my talking is inspired by you so there is no attachment. I want to think about when my talk is ok and not ok, and I imagine people accusing me of going against your instructions and I am preparing my defense. As I do all of this, I feel a busyness filling the head, and a sense of confusion and a fading away of your Voice. And so I recognize that I have identified with the mind. What do you have to say to me?*

Answer: As you set the purpose of letting go of attachment to mind, you can expect to become more aware of that attachment. It may seem that you have more attachment than before or that you are experiencing resistance, but in truth you are only noticing what you need to see if you are to break the attachment to mind and return to the recognition of Self.

It is ok that we go about this slowly. I am willing to talk slowly and take long breaks between points so you can continually break the attachment to mind and return your focus to me.

Identity with who you are will be helpful to this process. Every time you break the identification with mind you automatically identify with who you are, which will seem to be no thought about identity. When your identification is in this place, your attention is on me and you can hear me clearly.

Question for the Inner Teacher: *Have you got any tips for helping us break the attachment to mind?*

Answer: This is a work that must be done thoroughly and completely, so my recommendation is that you keep your attention patiently on the work.

I can speak to you all through the day in every situation and tell you how to see and how to respond and how to stay with me if you consistently remember to break the attachment to mind. But as soon as you identify with mind as you, you block me. I cannot assist you unless you break the attachment to mind. This is the meaning and true purpose of surrender.

"What would you like to tell me now?" is another helpful question. When you invite me to speak, you put mind aside. This is breaking the attachment to mind.

I can speak one line at a time throughout the day. You will not be able to write them all down, but one line at a time throughout the day is much more helpful to awakening than many lines in the morning followed by consistent attachment to mind throughout the day.

Question for the Inner Teacher*: I started to have the thought that I am scared I cannot do this, but then I questioned the "I" thought, and immediately the thought died.*

Answer: That is because you are aware that "I" is not your true Heart. When you are aware enough to question it, it must die. It dies in the light of true knowledge.

Comment from the Questioner*: I feel it would be easier to do this work if I did not move from this seat (the place where I sit when I write with Spirit).*

Inner Teacher's Response: What you are noticing is the need for discipline, but if you desire it enough, discipline goes with you everywhere because you carry the desire for discipline within you.

But if you want to spend more time sitting in this seat with me while you learn the practice of detaching from mind, you may do that. Whenever you are not called to be away from this seat, sit in this seat. It will be good practice for you. But when you are called away from the seat, get up from this seat and go. And take discipline with you. Having no real attachment to this seat is an important part of surrender.

Comment from the Questioner*: You've asked us not to talk about or think about the Self. . . .*

Inner Teacher's Response: I've asked you to question the "I" that is talking about or thinking about the Self.

When you are imagining that you know what abiding in Self is . . . or when you imagine that you know what stillness is or what surrender is or what now is like . . . you block the experience of what it really is by judging it. Your expectations, which have come from your imagination, become criteria that you believe in. Then you do not allow the experience to be, or do not let the guidance be, because you have already decided that it must be something else.

I ask you to drop all expectations and let the guidance or experience of the current moment be what you were not told through thinking or imagining (what) to expect. This is what I mean when I say listen only to me. I mean let go of attachment to the thinking and remembering and judging and imagining mind.

Do not think about what I have just said. Do not even think about who has said it. To think is to believe that you are the "I" in thought. And that "I" separates itself from everything it defines and thinks about.

The mind is always trying to not be here now. That is because I am here now. Truth is here now.

That is also because the ego is dependent on script-making for survival. Since the ego is not real, it must be made to be experienced. You make the ego through script-making . . . through imagining . . . which is thinking about the past and the future and circumstances which are not real.

Here and now without thinking is death to the ego because it is not script-making. It is script-living, because the script is being experienced and you seem to live within it, but script-living is not script-making. So here and now is certain death or ending to the artificial "I" that is ego.

How to Awaken From the Dream, Part Two

March 5, 2009

Today I want to tell you how to awaken from the dream. It isn't a mystery, and anyone can awaken when he is ready. He simply will not awaken until then, but his time dreaming can be spent preparing himself to be ready. This is the purpose of devotion. Devotion is willingly awakening to what has always been true by leaving everything else behind.

Devotion is a slow process. I do not mean to say it will take many, many lifetimes to wake up through devotion. I mean to say that devotion is a slow process now in every moment. It slows time by slowing the mind. And with practice, experience becomes richer. You might liken it to enjoying a full-flavored meal more when each bite is taken slowly and held in the mouth while you enjoy the richness of its flavor. This is how life becomes when the busyness of the mind is absent and does not interfere.

The mantra will help to slow the mind and pull focus inward, which is devotion. This is because the Heart is within, but the mind is without. When one is focused on the Heart, one sees all things from within. One enjoys all experiences from a point of certainty that is within. But when one is focused on the mind, one is focused without. Without is a delusion of chaos made by staying without and refusing to live from within.

So as you see, you do have a choice.

When one focuses within through devotion, life quiets. This happens because one is no longer entangled in the mesh of chaos without. And if one is no longer entangled in the mesh of chaos without, one is no longer a part of it, and so he is free from chaos and the confusing cries of chaos die for him.

I am telling you how to wake up from the dream, and that is to choose to live your life from within. When one lives from within he is no longer a part of the dream, and so it dies for him, and he awakens.

Question for the Inner Teacher: *Would you please speak to us about the experience of living from within part of time while also being pulled back into the dream?*

Answer: Well, this will not work. One cannot get out of a pool of water and then get in again without once again getting wet. If he wants to stay dry and know the warmth of the sun on his dry skin as his only condition, he must choose to stay out of the pool.

Comment from the Questioner*: But this is very hard for us.*

Inner Teacher's Response: That is only because you are not fully ready not to be wet.

Questioner*: What do you recommend for us?*

Inner Teacher: I recommend that you question your mind. When you feel it is hard to stay out of the pool ask, "Who is this 'I' that wants to remain wet?" You will notice it isn't the "I" that loves the warmth of the sun. And you will also know that the warmth of the sun is your truest desire, and so the "I" that seeks warmth must be your true I.

Questioner*: This is the same teaching I have been taught before. (I am remembering the "true desire" teachings in The Holy Spirit's Interpretation of the New Testament (NTI).)*

Inner Teacher: There are no other teachings, but there is the realization that all teachings are the same and only one teaching is true.

Questioner: *It is up to me.*

Inner Teacher: And it is up to God. Both teachings are one.

Questioner: *Thank you.*

s/Self-Inquiry

March 6, 2009

Today I would like to speak more on self-inquiry. We are introducing two inquiries: self-inquiry and Self-inquiry. The two are not the same. I will begin today by talking about self-inquiry.

"s"elf-inquiry is questioning the false "I" in order to recognize that it isn't truth. It isn't you. It is merely attachment to the mind. As self-inquiry makes the false "I" Self-evident, it is the decision of Self that breaks the attachment to mind and lays the current story to rest.

As self-inquiry is repeated over and over again, the attachment to mind is weakened just as the scratch of a razor blade weakens the strength of a rope. Eventually the razor blade works its way completely through the rope, and the attachment to mind is broken completely.

Some will also call this shining the light of awareness on an idea that is dark. When the light shines, it is darkness that disappears.

"S"elf-inquiry is different. Self-inquiry is a form of devotion where you incessantly seek the familiar, like seeking the familiar arms of the one you love. And you do not cease the seeking until you find her and are fully in her embrace assured that you can never lose her again. This is the purpose of Self-inquiry. It is seeking for the one you know.

Self-inquiry need not take a specific form. It is a desire . . . a devotion . . . that remains awake in you until the goal is satisfied. In fact, Self-inquiry has many forms and one seeker may use different forms at different turns along his path. But one thing is for certain and cannot be forgotten on the path of Self-inquiry. One must continually seek the true affection of his love, and he must not stop the seeking until he is certain it has been found.

Both self-inquiry and Self-inquiry lead in the same direction. The answer and destination are the same. You may use either or both. As your teacher, I will remind you to question the false attachment to mind and continually devote yourself to Self.

Comment from the Questioner*: I felt an inner prompt to pause from listening to the Inner Ramana and read from The Holy Spirit's Interpretation of the New Testament, NTI John, Chapter 3, verses 1-9. As I read I saw that this excerpt clearly describes the answer* *to self-inquiry and it also describes the destination of Self-inquiry. Here is that excerpt:*

> ***The Light is with man and the Light is in man, but the Light is not known by man unless he welcomes it. Each man welcomes the Light by his own choice and according to his own choice, but to know the Light fully, one must welcome it fully.***
>
> ***When a man welcomes the Light fully, he ceases to be a man, and he becomes the Light. For the Light is a presence that denies the existence of man; It knows only the Light. When a man becomes the Light, he is the Light, and he sings to all men of the Light, as he knows there is only Light.***
>
> ***This is what is meant by "to be born again." The existence you seemed to have before is gone, as if it never was, and the new existence is all there is and all there ever could be. It is seen in all places, in all directions and in all men, because it is truly all that can be seen.***[1]

After reading this I asked the inner teacher, "Is there anything else you would teach today?"

Inner Teacher's Response: Watch the mind for thoughts, which may be saying anything, but underneath the anything they say, they are truly saying, "I am thinking." Question, "Who is the 'I' that thinks?" and you will discover the belief in an individual and separate "I." That is the false "I," which exists only in thought.

1- The Holy Spirit's Interpretation of the New Testament: A Course in Understanding and Acceptance (NTI), The Foundation for the Holy Spirit

The Love of Discipline
March 7, 2009

Today I will talk about discipline.

Discipline is a dirty word to the mind. It screams "lack of freedom," "control" and extends ideas of being forced to do things you do not really want to do. But I ask you to look at the idea of "discipline" again and ask, "Who is the 'I' that has these ideas? Who is the 'I' that feels beaten down by the idea of discipline?"

Right now, it is as if two "I"s live within you. It is time we begin to look at these two "I"s now. One "I" is the false thought . . . the false idea of who you are. The other "I" is best described now as your true Heart.

One reason for learning the difference between these two "I"s is so you can learn to distinguish the difference between the "I" that speaks for what you want and the "I" that sounds like you, but in truth, it is an impostor.

Let's look again at the idea of discipline.

I have told you that discipline means consistency. You know that you want the consistent experience of God without end and without distraction, and you also know that consistent practice brings this experience. So you see, *you* love it. You are grateful for it. You want with your whole Heart to embrace it. It is the false "I" that wants to throw this idea away. It is the false "I" that resists and tells you that you hate discipline.

This is why it is helpful to question the false "I" thought that poses as you. This thought is literally an obstacle to the experience of Self. This false identification is everything that stands in the way of you knowing you. And if you continue to listen to it and continue to believe it as if its statements are your thoughts, then you continue to miss out on the experience of your truth.

The "I" thought must be questioned, and it must be seen that this thought isn't you.

Let's talk about the love of discipline.

Discipline is like a roadway lined with beautiful flowers and trees and green pastures to a destination that is literally more beautiful than your imagination. Who wouldn't want to take this road, and as they travel, embrace every moment of the beautiful and amazing journey?

This is discipline. It is consistently applying your devotion. It is lovingly loving your love. It is giving yourself exactly what you want.

Questioning the "I" thought that disagrees with discipline is like checking the map to make sure you don't leave this lovely road for a dry and dusty and bumpy one that heads off into the desert away from the lusciousness of your love.

"Follow your heart" is more than just a saying. When you can hear your true Heart calling, following your Heart is literally following a beacon home. And it will lead you there straightaway, if you remember that the beacon and the true "I" are one.

Truth Made Manifest
March 8, 2009

Today I will speak of guidance. More specifically, I will speak of God's guidance, which is the only guidance that is of concern to the mind that abides in Self.

Guidance is a word that is misunderstood, because it is believed that one can choose to follow guidance or choose not to. In fact, this is not the case. One is always following the guidance of the script or the guidance of karma. But one is not limited without free will to follow his guidance without choice. For there is the guidance of the "I" thought, which seems to be independent choice and decision making, and there is the guidance of God, which seems to come through surrender.

God's guidance is guidance that leads for the obviousness of Self. It guides in order to make truth manifest in form.

"I" thought guidance creates the illusion of non-truth. God's guidance is the obviousness of truth made manifest.

Today as you practice your devotion, I ask you to remember your desire to be an instrument of truth in this world. This is your desire to be fully surrendered . . . not at all attached to the "I" thought . . . so that the truth of God can be made manifest through you. Focus on this desire, and realize the power this desire has over you. Then surrender to this power, and let God walk the earth through you.

Extinguishment of "I" thought

March 9, 2009

When I say, "I am you," I speak the truth. And yet, I am not you as you know you in your thinking. This "you," which you call "me," is the idea that must be extinguished if you are to know me as you.

When I say the idea of "you" must be extinguished if you are to know me, many ideas run through your mind, none of which are true. Let's look at these ideas now.

When I say that "you" must be extinguished in order to know me, you think this will take a long time to do. This is not true. This is not true because the "you" that is being extinguished is only an idea, and the I that I am is living truth. In any moment, and then again in every moment, an idea can be extinguished so that living truth can be known.

It is true that if you are not finished with an idea, the idea that you desire can be reborn again in any moment. But it can also be extinguished once again, in any moment that you choose to put the false "I" aside and know living truth.

So as you see, it does not take time to extinguish a false identity. It only takes the desire to know living truth now.

Another idea that crosses your mind when I say you must extinguish "you" to know me is that this will be difficult. This is not true.

If you look at the idea, "This will be difficult," you will see it is only an idea. If you hold up the idea and shout that it is true, you are attached to the idea because you are holding to it. But if you let go of the idea, it will go away. The idea has no life, and so it can have no attachments. This idea is not attached to you; you are attached to it. If you let it go, it will go, because an idea cannot have a desire on its own that will cause it to stay.

It is true that if you are not finished with this idea, it will return to you. But if you can let it go once, you can let it go again. And in any moment that you are not holding to the idea, you can make the decision immediately to put aside the "I" thought, go into your Heart, and join with me.

Know yourself as your Heart, and you know me.

Another idea that crosses your mind when I ask you to extinguish "you" in order to know me is that extinguishing "you" means death. But when your mind is still and your attention is in your Heart, are you dead? Are you dead or are you aware? Are you dead or are you aware of your Heart, your love and your desire? Are you dead or are you more aware of *you* than you were when you were thinking and thinking (the) thinking was you?

I say you are not dead when you are aware of your Heart, your love and your desire. You are dead when you are not aware of these things. Therefore, the "you" that exists through identification with thought is not the "you" that is life. And if it is not life, extinguishing it cannot be death. To the contrary, it is birth into life, because you have walked out of death into awareness of life again.

I am your teacher, and as your teacher I will guide you to know what you already know. Move from your head to your Heart, and know that although you cannot define what you have found, and you cannot describe it, and you cannot use it to identify and differentiate you from anything else, that voiceless Voice and silent truth is your truth. And that is also the truth that I am.

The Mind that Thinks it is Lord
March 10, 2009

I want to speak to you today of confusion, and I want to speak to you of clarity. For confusion will keep you turning in circles and chasing your tail, seeking but never catching what you seek. Clarity leads you easily, slowly, like gliding, to the one goal that cannot be missed.

Confusion comes from judgment or deciding or thinking one knows without checking with me. This is the core of all confusion, and without this one error, confusion is impossible.

I ask you to look at this one paragraph (written above) and accept it deeply into your Heart. Do not think about it. Merely in peace and with love, accept what I say as true. Read the paragraph at least five times, silently accepting it before continuing.

Watch the mind carefully. Notice how it wants to judge my words or judge my methods. Notice how it wants to choose against me and decide what is best for itself. That is the confusion-mechanism. That questioning and doubting feature, which is a core mechanism within the mind, is a separation-creation mechanism that keeps you blind to the truth.

Read this paragraph (above) five times also.

Now you must ask, "Who is the 'I' that questions and doubts these teachings?"

Undoubtedly you will discover that it is an "I" that thinks it stands apart from these teachings.

So then ask, "Who is the 'I' that stands apart?"

There is no answer to this question, because there is no "I" that stands apart. If the mind should try to answer, "Me! I am the one who stands apart," ask the mind with conviction, "Who is 'me?'"

There shall be no answer, because there is no "I" that stands apart.

When the voice that questions and doubts my teachings has been put to rest, you will find the call in your Heart that asks you to simply and clearly listen to me, because I am the Voice of your Heart, and your Heart is the truth of what you are.

The humility you feel when you listen to your Heart is a true reflection of what we are, for there is no one above another and no one who can decide what is best for his Self.

Clarity comes when you listen to me without the questioning and doubting of mind. But in order to do this, the mind must be put to rest, because it is a natural function of the mind to question and to doubt and to want to decide for itself.

When you are listening to mind and you want to decide for yourself, you put yourself above me. When you are in this position of "above," you are identifying with a false perception of self. By false, I mean untrue, and so in that moment you are blind to Self.

"Abide in me as I abide in you" is a call to abide in the one Self where there is no one that stands and lords over another. But to know this one Self, you must put the lording-mind aside, because the mind that thinks it does know and it can decide does not know the one Self that at all times knows there is no lord.

A Contract for Awakening
March 12, 2009

What do you think I am teaching you?

Student Answers: *I understand that you want me to lay the individual thinking mind aside.*

Inner Teacher: I want you to see that it is nothing. And the Heart is everything.

The Heart is who you are and it is where all else springs forth from. When the Heart is seen as the source, that which springs forth is like the Heart. When it is believed that there is something else that can be a source, that which springs forth is like something else.

So we are here to get clarity on source, just as we are here to get clarity on Self, because they are the same. Belief in a different self . . . or mis-identification with the "I" thought . . . is also confusion about source. This is why it is said that ego is the cause of all suffering.

Student Asks: *What will you teach me now? Show me, that I may accept it.*

Inner Teacher: Your identification with the mind is the obstacle to knowing the beauty of your true Self. It is this identity that makes you blind. When you judge me and when you judge life by the mind's standards, you throw a blanket over the truth, and you choose not to see.

Read this paragraph (above) six times.

Student: *Ok. I have read it six times.*

Inner Teacher: It is important that you accept responsibility for your own path. I will lead you most deliberately now, but you must choose to follow just as deliberately. Do you agree to follow me and to do as I ask?

Student: *Yes, I agree to follow you and do as you ask.*

Inner Teacher: This may seem to be putting your self aside, but it is not, because the self that you call you is but an illusion of the mind. Therefore you put nothing aside.

The one who chooses to listen to me and follow me is the awakening of your true Self, so do not doubt your willingness to listen and follow me. That is you. And by listening to that desire, you listen to your Self.

Outside voices may seem to challenge your desire to follow me. Those outside voices will shout loudest in your own head. But do not question my teachings. Do not ask why. Do not ask for explanations of how it works. Just trust your Heart and follow me in devotion and love and desire to know your Self.

Student: *Alright, teacher. And what would you have me practice today?*

Inner Teacher: Practice all that I teach. Practice the mantra, and surrender, and the questioning of the "I" thought, and do it all through devotion. But most importantly, know your own inner devotion to these practices. Know your desire to practice them. Know your love and gratitude that such practices (gifts) should have been given. And know *that* love, *that* devotion, *that* desire *is* you, and listen to your Self.

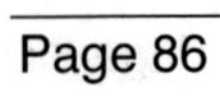

Pain and Purification

March 19, 2009

Question*: What is pain?*

Inner Teacher: Pain is nothing. When you ask the question, "What is pain?" you ask as if the answer is, "It is something." And you ask as if I can give you a special formula that will help you to permanently avoid this something you do not like. But I cannot give you a formula that will help you avoid something if that something is nothing. I can only ask you to trust me when I tell you it is nothing.

Questioner*: I feel what you are saying as you say it, and I can even feel the edge of realization that teaches pain is nothing. But I feel I need more. Please talk to me about pain and the practice of purification, and how all of this fits with your teachings.*

Inner Teacher: Purification seems necessary as long as you are identified with the false "I." For as long as you think you are it, you will also think that *you* are experiencing pain. But the key words in the previous sentence are "think" and "you."

Who is this "you" that experiences pain? Isn't it also the one who thinks? Isn't it also the mind that defines and separates? Is this mind what you are? And if not, then is it true that you are experiencing pain?

You see, the placement of your identity is more important than you may have previously thought it was. It is more important and more profound. If you place your identity with the false identity "I" in the thinking mind, then you experience everything it thinks up to prove that it exists. You are fully invested in it, and you fully experience all of its experiences. But this does not change the fact that you are not it, and it and the experiences that come from it are fully and perfectly illusion.

You see, the answer is this: The answer is to realize that it is not you. This is why s/Self inquiry works. As you realize the illusion is illusion, and it is not you, you are not affected by its dreams because you have found your Self to be beyond them and before them and above them. Your mind (attention) is anchored at a depth where they do not exist. Therefore, they touch you not.

Questioner: *Is the teaching of purification helpful at all (such as the teachings in The Holy Spirit's*

Interpretation of the New Testament, NTI 2 Timothy and NTI Revelation)?

Inner Teacher: Yes, all teachings are helpful as a part of the bridge, but the bridge is not the other shore. One must cross the bridge to the other shore and not remain on the bridge if he is to realize the beauty of the other shore.

Questioner: *How do we cross the bridge?*

Inner Teacher: By realizing you are not the false "I" who experiences illusion. You are the true Self, who is constant and changeless and sees the passing of all experience from a deep abidance within itself.

Questioner: *As sometimes happens when I am scribing, two words became mixed up in the sentence above. This is always corrected easily, and it happens when I am listening to one word that is ahead of the word I am writing. But in this case the error created something I would like to look at with you, since I feel deep within myself that it would be helpful.*

I was hearing the word "experience," which was to come later in the sentence, and I wrote this in error:

"You are the true Self, who is constant and changeless and experiences the passing of all experience . . ."

That's all the further the mistaken sentence went, because you showed me that I had attracted the word "experience" into the sentence too early. You showed me why it was an error and we corrected it. But only I saw this. Could we share in writing why this error was corrected?

> *(The error: "You are the true Self, who is constant and changeless and experiences the passing of all experience . . . "*
>
> *The correct sentence: You are the true Self, who is constant and changeless and sees the passing of all experience from a deep abidance within itself.)*

Inner Teacher: Experience is never constant. Experience is that which changes. Therefore, experience is not real or eternal as you are.

In the first writing of the sentence, it said that "Self experiences." This is not true. In order to experience, one would have to shift and change with experience. One would go up with happiness and down with depression, so to speak and as example. Self does not do this. Self is constant and changeless.

Self witnesses experience without changing and without being affected. Therefore, it is more correct to say that Self sees (or witnesses) experience than it is to say that Self experiences it. In fact, it is entirely incorrect to say that Self experiences. Self does not experience, and to say "I experience" is to identify with the false identification.

***Questioner**: And this is how purification is helpful, isn't it?*

Inner Teacher: Yes. In reality, purification is not necessary. Self is not affected and so Self cannot need purification. But one who is identified with the false "I" can begin to release attachment to false "I" thoughts, beliefs and experiences, because one who travels this road learns that he passes through the pain of purification and he emerges untouched. The untouched "I" that emerges is his true Self.

***Questioner**: So nothing was ever purified, but false identity or false attachment was seen to be untrue?*

Inner Teacher: Yes.

Questioner*: What do you recommend for those of us who are your students if we are still attached to mind enough to feel pain?*

Inner Teacher: I recommend you recognize what pain is. It signifies that you are attached to mind. And I recommend that you deal with pain, not by avoiding it, but by working on its root cause.

Look at thoughts of pain and ask, "Who is having these thoughts?"

Feel the emotions of pain and ask, "Why have these emotions arisen?"

If it is physical pain that you feel, notice the physical pain is centered in the body and ask, "What am I?"

Use the mantra that you are given to still the mind and return to the Heart. Practice devotion out of remembrance for what you are.

The Grace of the Guru
March 27, 2009

The teacher has come, and the teacher has come at the request of the student. Although the student did not consciously ask for this form of the teacher, this form has been given, because this form is a match to the Heart of the student.

Do not doubt that the teacher and student are one. The teacher merely speaks for the student, that she may see her own Heart more clearly.

It is as if I have come to abide in your Heart for a time. I have lit a campfire there and I sit by that fire singing the songs of the Heart. But that is only so you can hear yourself more clearly and recognize your Self above the chatter of the mind, so you may return to you there in the center of the Heart.

This is the grace of the guru. I light a little fire to shine a light on your home. But when you come, you light the chamber fully, for you are the light that *is* home.

Full-Time Inquiry for Self
March 28, 2009

The highest spiritual state is Self-realization. Nothing else matters. The mind may try to tell you that there are outward symbols of this internal state, and if you cannot achieve the outward symbols you are not realized. When the mind begins speaking in this way, inquire, "Who is the 'I' that speaks?" It is not the Voice of Self-realized.

Self-realization is all that matters, because when Self is realized nothing else affects it. Illness does not affect it. Poverty does not cause it harm. Loss of a friendship is no loss at all. The realized Self is full . . . full enough that it may allow the outward symbols to be what they may, and it does not lose its awareness of Self. Therefore, it does not lose its knowledge and awareness of love.

Make all things about one thing. Make every thought and every experience an opportunity to be aware of Self. Make this your only purpose, and Self-realization shall certainly become your reward.

Let nothing distract you from this one goal. Hold always to your practice. Seek the awareness of Self in all times and in all circumstances. Let finding Self be the only game that you play.

Seek Self before you go to sleep at night.

Let the search for Self
be the first thought when you awaken.

Inquire for the Self as you eat your meals.

Be aware of the Heart
as your hands are working.

As you recline, contemplate the Self.

As you walk, carry your Heart with you.

Never let your attention stray
from your love of Self or your inquiry of it.

Let this be your one purpose,
and live life fully.

Ask only for Self,
and awareness of Self shall be given.

The Only Choice is Where

March 30, 2009

The truth is that *all thought* rises out of the sense of "I" or because of the sense of "I," as a correction to this thought.

The state of true being precedes thought. Therefore, it is before thought, beyond thought and after thought. It is "no thought." And it scares you . . . seems to be death or nothingness to you . . . because you are identified *with thought*.

This is why people struggle against this idea so much. They believe the idea, "I think, therefore I am," which would mean that not to think would be to cease to exist. But this is not true. Thought springs forth from Existence. Existence is the birthplace of thought. Existence is not dependent on thought, and it never has been.

The idea "I decide" is an error. You choose to engage in the belief in thought, or you choose to observe thought without being engaged, or you choose to abide in Self completely and leave thought behind, but you do not decide what the thought will be.

Your choice is where, but not what. *What* is already in motion. But where you shall be while what does its thing is completely up to you, because the states of whereness are always available . . . always there for your choosing . . . no matter what is in the current moment.

This is why knowing your Heart is your only business. You do not decide what, so there is nothing about what that must be decided. You only choose where to be as what occurs, and where you want to be is not a question. You know where you want to be. Choose to be there, and you have complete alignment of will.

Be aware that the only choice is where, and make that choice in the moment according to the decision of the Heart.

Moving from Resistor to Abiding in Self
The final message in the Inner Ramana series

Regina: This message wasn't given as written message, so I can't read it to you. The message was given to me as the final message in this series. It was really the purpose for the entire series, and what I can do is explain that message to you.

In this particular message, the Inner Ramana taught me about three stages of mind. The three stages are resistor, doubter and abiding in Self.

The resistor is the most common stage in the world today. The resistor is when we think we know who we are.

Example:

I believe that I am Regina Dawn Akers.
I believe that I am a woman.
I know my age, when I was born, who my parents are, what I like, what I dislike . . .

This is the resistor. It is called "resistor" because all of these ideas are fully resisting the truth of what we are.

The second stage of mind is progressive towards awakening. It is called the doubter.

During the doubter stage, we are beginning to awaken. We are beginning to listen to truth about what we are. We may listen to this truth through a book, like *A Course in Miracles* or *The Holy Spirit's Interpretation of the New Testament*. We may listen to this truth through a teacher, like Ramana Maharshi. We may hear the truth within ourselves and speak to an inner teacher. But in all cases, even though we are beginning to recognize, listen to and practice the truth, we still feel we are learning the truth from an other. We feel we are the student and the book or the person or the inner guide is the one with the knowledge. It is the teacher, and we are learning what we did not know.

The reason this stage is called the doubter is because even though we are beginning to recognize our Self, we still doubt that it is our Self. Again, we think it is an other that is teaching us, the student.

The third phase of mind is called abiding in Self. This is when we are that Voice. We are that teacher. We are being it. We are fully identified with it. There is no longer any separation between me and what I truly am.

In the final message that I received from the Inner Ramana, I was told that I have had a healthy doubter phase. Doubter phase is a necessary bridge. Seemingly learning from a teacher is a natural process that we go through as we awaken to our Self. But I was also told that it was time for me to let go of the doubter phase and to begin to move into abiding in Self.

The tools that the Inner Ramana taught me . . . the mantra, surrender, self-inquiry . . . all of these tools were to be helpful to me in making this transition from doubter to abiding in Self.

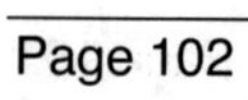

The Missing Ramana Message

Note: The following message was found on September 14, 2010 just prior to going to print with this book. The message was originally received on May 28, 2009.

The thinking that you are the self keeps you in a position of asking me questions. When this thinking is dead, questioning will also be no more. For knowledge is abundant, and you shall abide within abundant knowledge.

The doubter who asks and the resistor who does not ask are merely illusions of yourself . . . projections from a mind that does not know.

Who asks questions? And who answers them? And which one must be real, the questioner or the wise one who answers?

Resistance to asking . . . or the "I know" mind . . . is merely a cover over the mind that is forgetfulness. Therefore asking, or the state of doubting one's Self, is closer to realization than the total ignoring of Self. But one must put aside the doubter by resting in Self and being in Self. In this state, there are no questions, because you and Self are one.

The doubter doubts who he is, and so he questions. He questions as if he is another and somehow not his Self.

The shift from doubting to realizing occurs through resting in Self beyond doubting. Come without questions and simply be.

Closing

Regina: All of the messages that the Inner Ramana gave to me, I have taught. If anyone feels they would like to hear teachings along with the messages, you may go to www.reginadawnakers.com. There is an audio page dedicated to teachings from the Inner Ramana. Feel free to listen to those teachings as much as you like.

I also recommend listening to this audio and reading this book over and over and over again.